Second Declaration?

A Discussion on American Grievances

Todd Kos
7/15/2022

Table of Contents

This book is dedicated to America in hopes that it will convince people to be more politically active.

Chapter One: A Proposition; Division and War or Unity and Peace?

"When in the course of human events"….All Americans know this opening line. They know it's from the Declaration of Independence. They may even know a few more lines such as "We hold these truths to be self evident, that all men are created equal". But for majority of Americans that is it. The lucky few know a John Hancock refers to your signature and stems from the actual John Hancock signing his name first and boldly to the Declaration. As I said the lucky few. Most Americans don't know this document. If they were even lucky to read or have it read to them at all back in eighth grade they barely remember it. Even then, back in eighth grade, though they usually stopped at the most important part not even realizing it. Most people who read the Declaration believe the opening paragraph is the most important, or the body of the main text as a whole, in fact they often consider it to be the birth certificate of a nation and though not wrong it is far more than that. The truth is that the most important part of the document is the establishment of the right of government and the grievances, those complaints that the colonist held so strongly they compelled them to literally declare independence from the mother country. In fact the entire document was written for the sole purpose of presenting the grievances section in such a way that foreign entities and the people here in the colonies would support them and the cause of independence for America.

Why do I feel the study of the Declaration to be paramount to American society today, and who am I to believe this?

 America is by all metrics a divided nation. Ask members of political parties or independents and you will find many fear the direction of the country, and coming possible civil war or economic collapse. According to polls from Gallup to the Southern Poverty Law Center to almost every major media publication over the last three years the country is divided and many believe civil war is coming. Be it war between elements of the people and the central government in Washington DC, or War between the States and Washington DC. But many believe war to be coming. They see an America that is divided along political and religious ideology, sexual orientation, by race, color, creed, and most importantly between the growing wealth of the rich and the shrinking resources of everyone else in the country. They do not know what will spark the war, or along which lines fighting will be drawn, but they see the failing of America in the future. According to a survey by the Southern Poverty Law Center on June 1st 2022 53% of Republican respondents and 39% of Democrat believed the country was on course to a second civil war. What's even more troubling is the SPLC survey found that 44% of young people (Under 30) responding supported the idea of political assassinations. Even more surprising was the fact that when broken down by party affiliation it was majority Democrat youth supporting assassinations. In contrast almost a complete majority of respondents over 50 years of age were against assassinations for any reason regardless of party affiliation. Another poll done by the Washington Examiner at the end of 2021 found that 71% of Trump supporters saw civil war in the future with 40% of Biden supporters agreeing. Even if civil war or revolution doesn't come the metrics are clear, this country is divided. Who is to blame for that division?

 I am one of these Americans. I am not a scholar. I am not a professor. I am a common American Citizen struggling to maintain some semblance of middle class existence for myself and my family. I see the same divided America as my neighbors. It has made me think on the founding of this nation.

On the causes that compelled them not only to the separation but also to fight King and Country. What I see when I compare those claims of then and today is a central government rampantly out of control. If this is the case then is the central government to blame for the present state of disunion in America? Do we today have enough grievances to do what our ancestors did? Do we have more grievances potentially? What do we do if that is the case? That is the reason for the writing of this work. To ask these simple questions and to instruct my neighbors on the history of one of the greatest political documents in history the American Declaration of Independence.

Chapter 2: A Brief History

The Declaration was written by Thomas Jefferson but went through several revisions at the request of John Adams and Benjamin Franklyn as well as the Continental Congress itself. But once completed and agreed upon it is the document we know today. The total word count of the document itself is 1,337 words, and 56 individual signatures of the signers. Each signer was a member of the Continental Congress and represented the total of the 13 Colonies now declared States of America. The main recipient of the document was to be France in our push to gain French aid in our war with Britain. It was also widely distributed among the legislatures of the individual states, the military both Continental Army and State Militias, and the press. It received general support from among the American populace and overwhelming support of the British common people. Now an interesting fact, the time to disseminate the text of the actual Declaration meant that the furthest Colonies South Carolina and Georgia found out about the Declaration one to two months after July 4th. In fact papers in London England were publishing the text of the Declaration at the same time that rural Georgia was first hearing about it.

Independence Day in America is July 4th and actually celebrates the day that the Continental Congress adopted the Declaration in its final wording. The actual document everyone knows of especially if you have seen the movie National Treasure wasn't signed by the first signers until August 2nd. First the copy that is represented in the above movie had to be made. Essentially they needed to have an embossed version, the one displayed, for them all to sign. Second some states like New York didn't vote for independence on July 4th. They did so on July 9th as they were waiting on the response from the New York Legislature as to which way the vote on independence went. The letter had been delayed.

The Declaration is both a continuance upon the age old Magna Carta and also its own stand alone document. Where the Magna Carta established the right of a person's privacy and ownership over their own property, the Declaration establishes the right of the people to Life, Liberty, Pursuit of Happiness, and most importantly the Right of Government. This is the most important Right established by the Declaration. The Right of the people to both "establish" a government and too "abolish" a government. This is the key to the document. From there the grounds by which the people demanded grievances. Forget everything else and these are the most important.

When George Washington had the Declaration read to his army then in New York it lead to a riot as many patriotic Americans tore through the city destroying British statues and other propaganda. A statue of George the Third was torn down and subsequently melted into over 40,000 musket balls for the Continental American Army.

After being placed in Washington DC the Declaration has only moved two times in its history from the city, once during the war of 1812, and again during the Second World War. During the World War it spent the war at Fort Knox alongside the Constitution of the United States.

As for copies of the Declaration, after the adoption of the Declaration of Independence, the "Committee of Five"—Thomas Jefferson, John Adams, Benjamin Franklin, Roger Sherman and Robert R. Livingston—was charged with overseeing the reproduction of the approved text. This was completed at the shop of Philadelphia printer John Dunlap. On July 5, Dunlap's copies were dispatched across the 13 colonies to newspapers, local officials and the commanders of the Continental troops. These rare documents, known as "Dunlap broadsides," predate the embossed version signed by the delegates. Of the hundreds thought to have been printed on the night of July 4, only 26 copies are known to survive. Most are held in museum and library collections, but three are privately owned. Most recently one was found at a garage sale in 1989 held in the back of a picture frame. The Dunlap was in almost perfect condition and sold at auction in 2000 for 8.1 Million dollars. The picture frame it was found in cost 4 dollars at the garage sale.

The price of this history is priceless as proven by the shear amount people will pay to simply hold a piece of it. The formation of America is the like of something that has never happened before or after. No other revolution in history was as successful as the American Revolution, nor as permanently lasting. The debate as to why has raged for the entire history of this nation. For some it's the fact that this was the first revolution to be started from a government, the governments of the 13 colonies. For others it's the tenacity

and perseverance of George Washington and
the American Continental Army. Even others
blame the King of England and his frivolous
spending. Regardless all agree that without
the Declaration of Independence it would not
have been successful.

Chapter 3: Original Grievances

"A decent respect to the opinions of mankind requires that they should declare the causes which impel them to the separation"…The true purpose of the Declaration the grievances with Great Britain. First what is a grievance? Well according to the Oxford dictionary as of the writing of this work it is "the infliction of wrong or hardship on a person". The Declaration of Independence list 27 agreed upon grievances. To truly understand the document in its entirety one must know the grievances to which the document was written for. They are as follows with short explanations. Also please note that the reference of "He has" is in reference to King George the Third who was King of England at the time of the American Revolution.

1) **"He has refused his Assent to Laws, the most wholesome and necessary for the public good."**

As before mentioned the American Revolution was unique in that it came from a position of Government. Each of the 13 colonies already had their own legislatures much like the state governments of today. These legislatures already handled majority of the daily legal needs of the individual colonies. The colonies had been petitioning for the right to have their own representatives elected to the British Parliament or for the establishment of an American Legislature which would handle the duties usually prescribed to Parliament for the American continent. Having been refused the King had attempted to disband or legally castrate the local colonial legislatures. The King had a repeated history of failing to ratify legislation of the colonial legislatures making it increasingly harder for the government of the colonies to provide for the public good of the individual colonies. Self Governance would become the central point and reason for the revolution and the subsequent Declaration of Independence.

<u>2)</u> He has forbidden his Governors to pass Laws of immediate and pressing importance unless suspended in their operation till his Assent should be obtained; and when suspended, he has utterly neglected to attend to them

During the time of the revolution the leading political philosopher to influence colonial leaders was John Locke. Locke believed we were born from a position of freedom. That our natural state of existence was to be free. He said that people come together and form unions such as government

to ensure the protection of these freedoms. To
Locke neglect was a justifiable cause to establish
new government. The neglect of those in positions
of power leads to the diminishing freedoms of the
people and is against the natural state of a free
persons being. So for the King to neglect the needs
and will of the colonist was tantamount to
establishing a slave state.

_3)_ **"He has refused to pass other Laws for
the accommodation of large districts of
people unless those people would
relinquish the right of Representation in
the Legislature, a right inestimable to
them and formidable to tyrants only."**

In John Lockes book "Two Treatises of
Government" he states "When such a single
person, or prince, sets up his own arbitrary will, in
place of the laws, which are the will of the society,
declared by the legislative, then the legislative is
changed" The concept here is that without a
position from which the will of people is to be
heard, the legislature, then the people are slaves or
property of the state. As the founders believed in
the free state of being at birth then this concept of
property of the state was egregious and
reprehensible. To be made property of the state

meant to have no individual rights or individual sovereignty.

> *4)* **"He has called together legislative bodies at places unusual, and also uncomfortable, and distant from the depository of their Public Records, for the sole purpose of fatiguing them into compliance with his measures."**

When the British closed the port of Boston after the infamous Boston Tea Party where tons of British tea was thrown into the harbor by patriots disguised as Native Americans the appointed royal governor Thomas Gage caused a number of acts to be passed by Parliament. One of these acts allowed for the dissolution of the Massachusetts Charter of 1691 which allowed Gage to disband the legislature in 1774. These acts of Gage's lead to other governors disbanding their colonial legislatures as well, for example the royal governor of Virginia at the time John Murray Earl of Dunmore dissolved the House of Burgesses, Virginia's colonial legislature, as well in 1774. These disbandment's and dissolutions caused the legislatures whom feeling since they were elected by the people of the colonies to meet in places that were often isolated and far from the workings of government. It would fuel the fire for independence as many revolutionaries believed America both could and should govern itself.

<u>**5)**</u> **"He has dissolved Representative Houses repeatedly, for opposing with manly firmness his invasions on the rights of the people."**

This grievance follows the thread of the previous. Continuing upon the complaint that they were forced to meet away from the halls of government, the government of the King had attempted to make the elected legislatures abandon their constituency. It started in 1768 when Massachusetts wrote a letter to the other colonial assemblies and legislatures urging them to support a united front against England that Great Britain had no right to tax the colonies without colonial consent. This is where the phrase "No taxation without representation" was born. King George in response threatened the colonial governments with dissolution or disbandment if they followed Massachusetts and united as one. Over the course of the next six years the different legislatures would face numerous challenges to their rightful authority from both the crown and Parliament.

<u>**6)**</u> **"He has refused for a long time, after such Dissolutions, to cause others to be**

> **elected; whereby the Legislative Powers,
> incapable of Annihilation, have returned
> to the People at large for their exercise;
> the State remaining, in the meantime,
> exposed to all the Dangers of Invasion
> from without, and convulsions within."**

In the same train of complaints as grievance four
and five but with a different perspective on the
problem at hand, here the colonist were attempting
to show he didn't just dissolve and disband he also
prevented new government from being established
so as leaving the people of the colonies without the
security of an ordered state.

7) **"He has endeavored to prevent the
population of these States; for that
purpose, obstructing the Laws for
Naturalization of Foreigners; refusing to
pass others to encourage their migrations
hither and raising the conditions of new
Appropriations of Lands."**

With the end of the French and Indian War,
America saw an increase of immigration to its
shores, especially from Germany, and the Dutch.
These peoples were not Anglican Church members
or British citizens, and came from regions with
progressive views on both religion and politics. To

stem this tide of immigration the King George the Third first made an agreement with certain native tribal nations like the Cherokee Nation and the Iroquois Confederacy to not allow immigration west beyond the Appalachian Mountains. This prevented westward expansion beyond the mountains and into the Ohio River Valley. This angered the colonist as they had just fought a seven year war over these lands with or alongside as well as against many of the tribes negotiated with by England. In conjunction he made the acquiring of new land in approved regions of the frontier more expensive via government regulations, fees, and taxes. Finally he suspended the right of colonial legislatures to issue nationalization papers to immigrants forcing the question of new citizenship back to England where the King refused to address the issue.

_8)_ **"He has obstructed the Administration of Justice by refusing his Assent to Laws for establishing Judiciary Powers."**

By 1774 the King and Parliament had suspended the colonial Judiciary of Massachusetts removing all serving elected judges and appointing his own. He also refused to allow the people to enact any judicial reforms of their own. The same act of Parliament also suspended to right of trial by jury so the administration of justice was considered to be obstructed. Other colonies voiced similar complaints at the time of the Declaration of Independence, thus its inclusion in the list of grievances.

9) **"He has made Judges dependent on his Will alone for the tenure of their offices, and the amount and payment of their salaries."**

As mentioned in the last grievance the colonist had been prevented from the right to appoint or elect their own judges and officials. This would also mean they weren't responsible for the salaries of these individuals. The King paid the salaries of the judges and colonial governors But these salaries were paid out of taxes collected by the crown from the colonist and colonies. The colonist believed that since governors and judges were dependent on the king for both their salaries and instructions these individuals had no interest in listening too or supporting the colonies or colonist in any way. This grievance is found to be the reason for the establishment of the Colonial Committees of Correspondence. The Committees were formed in late 1760's in a successful attempt by the colonies to one remain in contact with each other and their agents in England subverting the Kings attempts to disrupt colonial self government and organization, and two to act as shadow governments within each of the 13 colonies in the event that the King or Parliament disbanded a colony legislature. Many people by the start of the revolution believed the committees to have more power than the actual colonial legislatures.

> ***10)*** **"He has erected a multitude of New Offices and sent hither swarms of Officers to harass our people and eat out their substance."**

The Stamp Act and the subsequent suspension of the colonial judiciary lead to the creation of lots of new royal offices in the colonies. The Stamp Agents were charged with collection of the taxes and fees associated with receiving tax stamps and issuing those stamps. When the judiciary was suspended in different colonies the court of the admiralty and vice admiralty were created and began handling judicial trials. All of these royal agents received their funding or salaries from the crown but those salaries which were quite substantial were collected ultimately from the money made off the colonies. This is why they added the part about eating out their substance. These taxes and salaries were financially devastating the colonies. The burden on the colonist to fund the salaries meant the kings agents were ruthless and callous in the performing of their duties. This grievance holds true for many Americans even today as our own government has created a multitude of unelected bureaucratic offices filled with agents and officers of the central government whom receive large salaries and benefits packages.

11) **"He has kept among us, in times of peace, Standing Armies without the Consent of our legislatures."**

With the end of the French and Indian War standing troops became a common sight in certain colonies. As problems with the colonist progressed and especially after the dissolution of so many colonial legislatures more troops were sent from England and raised from amongst the colonist. These troops supported the needs of the Kings agents, and enforced the will of the Kings appointed Military Governors such as General Gage in Philadelphia and Boston. These troops were brought over by order of the King and Parliament or by request of the Royal Governors not by the Colonies themselves.

<u>*12)*</u> **"He has affected to render the Military independent of and superior to the Civil Power."**

After Massachusetts government was suspended Gage was appointed both Military Governor and Commander and Chief of all British forces in North America he was granted power over the running of the Massachusetts government, the collection of taxes and duties, and the enforcement of law in the colony/ies. He endeavored to make soldiers subject to military law only preventing the civil authority to prosecute or persecute soldiers who violated the rights of colonist, and he refused to allow any civilian oversight of the criminal or civil courts of the admiralty he had established.

<u>*13)*</u> **"He has combined with others to subject us to a jurisdiction foreign to our constitution, and unacknowledged by our laws; giving his Assent to their Acts of pretended Legislation:"**

As each of the colonies had been founded under charters which established the colonial governments many of the colonist believed that meant they were entitled to the right of self governance and self determination. They believed that since they were not allowed in Parliament and that Parliament had no jurisdiction over the colonies as that right was entitled to the colonies via their founding charters. This meant the colonist considered Parliament to be a foreign power and entity to that of the established and approved governments of the colonies.

_14)_ "For quartering large bodies of armed troops among us:"

As General Gage increased the number of troops in the colonies these soldiers had to be housed. In Europe the common practice was to quarter troops with civilians if no other accommodations were available. As the colonies were still young majority of the building projects had been for development of the civilian infrastructure not military. After the end of the French and Indian war there was no longer any major power in the continental north that could threaten the colonies so the colonist did not feel the need to build forts and redoubts to house large quantities of troops. As Gage brought more and raised more soldiers he had to house them. Instead of building military barracks he chose to do as Europe had done for generations when space was needed and quartered the troops among the populace. Most without any compensation, meaning soldiers were eating colonist food, and utilizing colonist resources

further draining the colonial reserves. The Colonist
felt this to be a direct violation of the age old
Magna Carta and the rights of private property, and
that it was a drain on the colonist financially.

15) "For protecting them, by a mock Trial
from punishment for any Murders which
they should commit on the Inhabitants of
these States:"

In the year 1768 two colonist citizens were killed
by British troops in Maryland after a dispute
ensued. The soldiers were tried via the Admiralty
Court not a civilian court, and without a jury only
the agents of the King to preside over the trial.
Despite overwhelming and damning evidence
against the soldiers in question they were acquitted.
Naturally the colonist were outraged, the Kings
men could murder civilians. The colonist had no
legislatures or courts. They were truly being
enslaved by the crown or so they rightly felt.

16) "For cutting off our Trade with all parts
of the world".

After the French and Indian War tensions between
France and England as usual in their history
remained high. This lead to Parliament passing
what would be known as the Navigation Acts.
These acts controlled how, when, and who England

and her subject colonies could trade with. As a result many of the French and Spanish colonies in the Caribbean, Louisiana territory, and Central and South America were off limits. This hurt the American colonies immensely. Coffee for example which had become quite popular in the colonies with the boycotts of tea mainly came from the Spanish Colony of Florida. Also Colonial hard woods were highly sought after in those foreign colonies for building and production. Not to mention cotton, and tobacco especially by the French, and of course America wanted French or Spanish sugar out of Louisiana or Cuba as it was cheaper than the Portuguese sugar out of Brazil. The Colonist had no animosity toward these powers and didn't believe that England's age old hatreds should inhibit the colonies or their economy. They also felt the Acts were a direct attack against the colonist themselves as to support their boycotts they had increased trade with both France and Spain.

17) "For imposing taxes on us without our consent:"

"Taxation without representation" the revolutionary cry that most Americans do actually know came about not just because of one act or one tax but a host of taxes imposed over the course of many years. Rightly the colonist believed they should not be taxed by Parliament and the King without having been represented in the Parliament. They took the imposition of these taxes as a direct assault on the sovereignty and self direction of the colonial governments. The tax acts that most infuriated the colonies were the Molasses Act of 1733, the Currency Act of 1764, the Sugar Act of 1764, the Stamp Act of 1765, the Townsend Acts of 1767 which were also known as the Intolerable Acts by the colonist, and the Tea Act of 1773. There were others but these were the main ones the colonist complained over. England claimed these taxes were needed to fund the defense of the colonies, and repay the crowns debts incurred from the French and Indian War. Colonist countered that they had helped to fund and supply the war effort which based on historical records does show the colonies suffered significant cost for the war they were never compensated for and that they could defend themselves without need of British troops as their militia were instrumental as well to winning that war. They also argued that Parliament refused to reign in the uncontrollable spending of the crown.

_**18)**_ **"For depriving us in many cases, of the benefit of Jury trial:"**

After the dissolution of the Massachusetts colonial government in 1768 Parliament passed another act whereby violations of revenue and tax law fell under the jurisdiction of the Admiralty Courts where no jury was required, and the agents of the courts who were the Kings agents were biased toward England. Rightly the colonist declared this to be a violation of their rights to fair justice and to be judged by a jury of their peers.

_19)_ "For transporting us beyond Seas to be tried for pretended offenses:"

In 1774 Lord North introduced an act to Parliament called the "Administration of Justice Act" where any colonist accused of capital offenses, murder, rioting, resistance to British law or agents, or resisting revenue and tax laws in any way or degree could at the behest of the governor be shipped to a different colony or all the way back to England to stand trial. To make it worse evidence was not required to deport someone the simplest accusation of a British agent or soldier was all that was needed to move forward and petition the governor.

_20)_ "For abolishing the free System of English Laws in a neighboring Province, establishing therein an Arbitrary government, and enlarging its

In the year 1774 Parliament passed the Quebec Act which increased the size of Canada allowing for Canadian expansion, where the colonies had instead been limited by agreements between the crown and native tribes. It also established French Common Law instead of British over the whole of Canada which granted more power to the crown than British law. Lastly it allowed the French descent Catholics of Canada to practice openly and freely the Catholic Religion, where in turn the colonist, were being limited to the Anglican church of England publicly and their own faiths privately. The belief in the colonies was that this would enlarge the powers of the King and in time be forced upon their own colonies as well.

<u>**21)**</u>

By the year 1774 majority of the individual founding charters of the 13 colonies had been dissolved and disbanded by acts of Parliament and the King. This had the effect of turning the colonies into despotic states under the tyranny of the King George the Third and his agents.

22) "For suspending our Legislatures and declaring themselves invested with power to legislate for us in all cases whatsoever".

The dissolution of colonial charters brought about the disbandment of colonial legislatures. This meant only the Kings governors, and agents had the power to legislate, enforce laws, and collect taxes or revenue. This grievance though technically listed by association with the last grievance was important for the colonist to show that they had been arbitrarily enslaved under a system of despotism whereby they had no rights of self government.

23) "He has abdicated Government here, by declaring us out of his Protection and waging War against us."

In 1775 King George the Third addressed the Parliament and declared the colonist to be in an open state of rebellion against the crown and mother England. Parliament then passed the Prohibitory Act which effectively ordered the shutting down of all trade between the colonies and

the colonies trade with England. When combined
with Navigation Acts this was effectively a
declaration of economic war on the colonies by
England. The King also used this act to send more
soldiers to the colonies with the power to enforce
all laws and subjugate all resistance, as well as
negotiate with Native Tribes to provide men to
assist the army against the colonist and to negotiate
the employ of German Hessian mercenaries for use
in the colonies as well. The use of the savagery of
the Natives style of war and the Hessians being
considered the most ruthless troops in all of Europe
convinced many colonists that England had no
desire for peaceful resolution of differences with
the colonies and only war would be of use now in
dealing with England. These acts were the final
straw for many colonist who had until now been on
the fence about rebellion against England.

24) **"He has plundered our seas, ravaged our coasts, burnt our towns, and destroyed the lives of our people."**

In the years leading up to the Revolution Lord
Dunmore whom had served as both Royal
Governor of Virginia as well as New York was a
staunch supporter of the crown and Parliament. He
is the governor whom tried to deny colonial access
to militia arms and weapons, and ordered the

seizure of suspected patriot merchant ships and the naval assaults on coastal town and ports believed to be supporting the patriot colonial cause. It was he who ordered the assault on Falmouth where by the British Navy shelled the town for nine hours using a combination of shot including incendiary. The winter stores were hit and burned to the ground. This was the biggest act of retaliation against towns and ports that supported patriot causes by the crown and his governors.

_**25)**_ **"He is at this time transporting large Armies of foreign Mercenaries to complete the works of death, desolation, and tyranny, already begun with circumstances of Cruelty & Perfidy scarcely paralleled in the most barbarous ages, and unworthy the Head of a civilized nation."**

The employ of Hessian mercenaries out of Germany was one the greatest blunders of George the Third. This act more than any other solidified colonial resolve. Hessians were considered the most brutal troops in all of Europe. They were known to use bayonets on the wounded and surrendering enemies in direct violation of all rules of war. They were known to use dishonorable tactics such as civilian shields, and threatening children to achieve order. They were made up of ranks of indentured soldiers who faced death if they refused orders or deserted so they fought with a ferocity akin to in colonial minds the Native Tribes of America whom many colonist feared.

> ***26)*** **"He has constrained our fellow Citizens taken Captive on the high Seas to bear Arms against their Country, to become the executioners of their friends and Brethren, or to fall themselves by their Hands."**

By an act of Parliament in December of 1775 the British Navy was authorized to seize American merchant ships supporting the patriots, but instead of imprisoning the crews as prisoners of war they were impressed conscripted into the navy and army fighting against the colonist. This meant they were forced upon pain of death to fight their own colonial countrymen.

> ***27)*** **"He has excited domestic insurrections amongst us and has endeavored to bring on the inhabitants of our frontiers, the merciless Indian Savages whose known rule of warfare, is an undistinguished destruction of all ages, sexes, and conditions."**

This grievance is one of the most debated in modern circles. The colonist had been wanting to expand West since before the start of the French and Indian War all those years ago, but since the war, the agreements of the King with the Native Tribes had prevented it. With the start of the Revolution British agents convinced many tribes that their treaty with England meant they had to support the British war effort. The employ of Natives against the colonist was seen to be as dishonorable an act as hiring Hessian mercenaries.

Chapter 4; Discussions on the state of modern affairs as compared to the grievances of the Colonist.

Today America is as we have already established a divided nation. The people are found to be in many overlapping camps of thought and belief. Since the 1960s Americans have used the first amendment to force attempted reforms to women's rights, racial relations, sexual identity and preference, to support or protest wars and foreign involvement, for political candidates and causes, and a host of other topics. Americans are good at action but we unfortunately on average fail on the follow through. We achieve victory in the moment then fail to remain vigilant. The establishment government waits until we are onto the new fad or craze. Then they manipulate what was achieved for their own ends. One cannot expect less of government. One can expect more from the people. Government by its very nature wants to grow. It is the job of the people to remain vigilant and limit government growth to where and when needed for the needs of society. Republics being advanced government doesn't just want to grow it needs to for its very survival but that growth can be limited and directed by the will of the vigilant populace.

The major topics facing America at the time of this writing are:

1) Growing and uncontrollable inflation
2) High Taxes
3) Government Spending and Malfeasances
4) Government Regulations and Regulatory Agencies
5) Second Amendment and Firearm Rights
6) Reproductive Rights
7) Medical Rights
8) Gender Identity Rights
9) Foreign Entanglements
10) Foreign Investment
11) Private Central Banking
12) Infrastructure
13) Education
14) Land Rights
15) Immigration
16) Border Security
17) Religious Rights
18) First Amendment Free Speech Rights
19) Growing Central Government
20) Diminishing Local and State Government
21) Fourth Amendment Rights of Privacy and Government Intrusion
22) Fifth and Sixth Amendment Rights as compared to Policing Rights and Authority

23) The unaccountable Murder of American
   Citizens at home or abroad
24) Economic Malfeasance
25) And a host of topics not listed

Now this is a simple list. There are other topics as well and even those listed here are far more complex than a simple point on a list. They are vast with numerous sides quarrelling over whose beliefs, philosophy, and ideology is superior to addressing the cause at hand. Regardless you see in this list a semblance of the grievances of yester year and the original Declaration of Independence. Taxes, Government overreach, free speech, diminished local government, murder of citizens, judiciary complaints, foreign complaints, trade or economic complaints all can be found today as they were back then. Though they may not be exactly the same in every instance some may be eerily similar.

No one can deny that inflation in 2022 is rampant though many debate on the reasons as to why. Yes there was a global pandemic but unfortunately for the establishment leaders of the world the numbers of dead were made greater in every metric by their interference rather than letting it run its course as many experts suggested and several nations proved to be the right decision. In fact Scientific America ran an article in March of 2021 detailing the many failings of the government during the pandemic response. This article entitled How the US Pandemic Response went wrong and what went right.

https://www.scientificamerican.com/article/how-the-u-s-pandemic-response-went-wrong-and-what-went-right-during-a-year-of-covid/

One cannot discount government spending which has ramped up on average year after year since the fall of the Soviet Union. The United States establishment government in Washington DC runs this country on a deficit spending program whereby year after year we run up more and more debt so that today the debt exceeds Thirty Trillion US dollars. The Annual deficit which is still rising every minute of every day is in excess One Trillion Six Hundred Million. The Deficit is the money the government must borrow and does not have on hand. This is the yearly addition to the National Debt. To be so exceedingly in debt puts the livelihood of every American Citizen in a state of constant threat. Should nations decide to stop using the Petrol Dollar ie the US dollar for international transactions or switch to a universal digital income we the people are left holding the bill with a worthless dollar going the way of the Weimar

Republic of pre Nazi Germany and it costing a thousand dollars a loaf of bread. Since our dollar is not backed by specie of any kind as constitutionally required and ignored by the central government we do not have a reserve to fall back on as England did when the Pound Sterling lost its place as the reserve currency of the world after World War 2. America and her people would be devastated. For some reason our leaders don't seem to care. They are either oblivious to the feelings in the world toward America today by their years of constant foreign entanglements. Perhaps they see the writing on the wall and are trying to get as big of piece of the pie before the collapse. Or could they be purposely devaluing and weakening the United States for some globalist corporate Banker agenda as many in alternative media or private free press have suggested. People like Alex Jones with Info Wars, William Cooper, Joe Rogan, and Joel Skousen to name a few. One simply need research the polls of trending topics today to see the varying view points and main stream beliefs.

We can definitely establish private grievances today but what of the states? They have failed to give the territorial lands to the new states formed since the civil war of the 1860's endeavoring to force those states to acquiesce to the central government. This can be researched today by looking up the topic the Sage Brush Rebellion and the Bundy Ranch Fiasco. They have through the central bank the private Federal Reserve dominated the potential finances of the fifty states and forced them into being subservient to federal grants and finances. They have grown federal regulatory agencies granting more and more control to the central government over the individual state economies these agencies include but are not limited to the FBI, EPA, OSHA, FDA, CDC, Etc. Now though these agencies do provide some good they are also responsible for some the greatest central government screw ups in the last Fifty years. They have accepted deals from foreign powers which directly affect the 50 states without the ratification of the Senate. Research the Smart City Initiative, or George HW Bush signing onto the UN Agenda 21 plan when he visited Rio de Janeiro Brazil. Another source of information on these topics can be found via the Trilateral Commission reports, World Economic Forum, Council on Foreign Relations, Davos, or the G7 summits. Research these organizations and their publications to see what the governments of the Western NATO world are planning in years to come. All the governments within NATO meet with and have arrangements with these organizations. Leaders of these nations often go to the yearly meetings for these organizations and some free press outlets claim they divulge state secrets from time to time. If true for any of our leaders that the revealing of state secrets is a violation of constitutional law and a risk to national security possibly even treason.

I believe we have established that there are grounds to write if not act on a second Declaration. Why write one if not to act on it? By writing it we can use it to help show our grievances. Perhaps wake up or motivate Americans to see past the daily problem and look to bettering the future as a whole. Mostly though we can use it as a guide for the state governments to one elect the right people to office who stand with us and not the corporations or political party, two we can use it as guide by which to direct our state governments to challenge the authority and over reach of the central government. If need be and in the most extreme situation should the tyranny of Washington DC become greater and not less as was the folly of the George the Third so long ago we can use it as a base from which to write an official state accepted Declaration to restore the Constitution and will of the people to the central government. Though I pray we in America can rise above the less civilized way to handle things. The great German tactician and military theorist Carl von Clausewitz wrote 'War is a mere continuation of policy by other means." Meaning War and the Military are but extensions of politics when diplomacy or dialogues have failed. Let us hope we in America never stop trying to talk to one another.

Chapter 5; A New Declaration

For the purpose of this writing I will not be coming up with an entirely new Declaration body but instead will endeavor to rewrite the original to fit the times and grievances of today. For a complete original text please check the appendix of this work or the National Archives at

The Declaration of Independence | National Archives

And though this is a slight rework for those familiar with the original document I encourage you to read it all the way through for though the changes are slight they are also dramatic in their own way. Also in the list of grievances "They" is in reference to the Central Government.

The Unanimous Declaration of the People of the 50 Sovereign States of America

When in the course of Human Events it becomes necessary for one people to dissolve the political bands which have connected them to another, and to assume among the powers of the Earth, the separate and equal station to which the laws of nature and Natures God entitle them, a decent respect to the opinions of mankind requires that they should declare the causes which impel them to the separation.

We held these truths to be self evident in 1776, and we still hold them to be true today. That all people are created equal, that they are endowed by their creator with certain unalienable rights, that among these, though not limited to, are Life, Liberty, Privacy, Individual Sovereignty, Due Process, Honest and Accountable Government, and Pursuit of Happiness. That to secure these rights governments, are instituted among the people, and by the people, deriving their just powers from the consent of the governed.

That whenever any form of government becomes destructive of these ends it is the right of the people to Alter or to Abolish it, and to institute new government, laying its foundations on such principles, and organizing its powers in such form, as to them shall seem most likely to effect their security and happiness. Prudence indeed will dictate that governments long established should not be changed for light and transient causes and accordingly all experience has shown that mankind are more disposed to suffer while evil is sufferable, than to right themselves by abolishing the forms to which they are accustomed. But when a long train of abuses and usurpations, pursuing invariably the same object to reduce the people under absolute globalist despotism, and financial tyranny, it is not just the peoples Right, it is their Duty to throw off such government and to provide new safe guards for their future security.

Such has been the patient sufferance of these Fifty Sovereign States of the Union, and their sovereign citizens. Such is now the necessity which constrains them to seek to restore the rightful Constitution from would be Usurpers, entrenched in the halls of the central government in Washington DC.

The history of the present Washington Establishment Government is a history of repeated injuries and usurpations all having in direct object the establishment of an absolute tyranny over these Free States and People.

To prove this let facts be submitted to a candid world;

1) They have failed to provide for the moral good instead endeavoring to play one group of Americans off another in hopes of fomenting chaos and enlarging the powers of the Central Government. Time and again politicians have riled up masses of people by withholding the Full Truth and endeavoring to guide them through fear instead of up front honest leadership as is expected by the constituency and required by the Oath of Service.

2) They have planned as well as orchestrated false flag attacks on their own people, the citizens of the United States

3) They have murdered their own citizens by
unmanned drone strikes on foreign soil and
through the use of federal law enforcement
at home

4) They have orchestrated riots and
insurrection against many of the States

5) They have privatized the powers of the
people entrusted to them by the people and
the fifty States shirking the duties entrusted
to them to unelected oligarchs and private
investors.

6) They have in direct violation of the
Constitution created a system of fiat
currency removing the constitutionally
mandated specie backing the peoples
money, robbing the peoples value, wealth,
sovereignty, and pursuit of happiness in a
despotic attempt to enslave the people in a
system of debt and dependence on the
Central Government.

7) They have failed and continue to fail year
after year to balance the budget of the
United states of America running up the

national debt through yearly deficit
spending endangering the future security of
America, her citizens, and the fifty States

8) They would rather raise the debt ceiling
year after year than rain in their
uncontrolled spending

9) They have failed to keep many States and
municipalities solvent financially due to
their fiat system

10) They have sold the peoples landmarks and
historical sites to foreign powers after
taxing the people to build and maintain and
continuing the taxing the people for that
maintenance even after sale

11) They have used their control of the global
economy via the fiat petro dollar reserve
currency they created and forced on the
world to punish those nations that do not go
along with their vision of global world
order never caring for the consequences to
their own citizens economy and trade

12) They have enacted a host of unelected
bureaucratic offices and sent agents hither
to, to eat out the peoples substance. Time
and again they divulge their powers
entrusted to them to regulatory agencies
that write regulation then enforced with the
writ of law though the peoples
representatives never voted on them. Time
and again these regulations endeavor to
indebt the people in the system of fiat
currency unconstitutionally created by
those in
Washington.

13) They place over the decision process of
these regulatory agencies boards filled with
members who have conflicts of interest be
it financial or personal that effect the
decision making process with no
requirements to recues themselves when a
conflict of interest occurs

14) They allow High Ranking Military officers
to be courted by weapons and other arms
manufacturers so these officers are invested
in and often upon retirement consult for
these same corporations, all this endeavors
to make these officers dependent on the

manufacturers and creating a conflict of interest in military contracts and research grants

15) They have failed to properly educate the youth of America causing each successive generation since the founding of the Department of Education to be less informed, less knowledgeable, and less capable than the preceding generations

16) They are endeavoring to rewrite history to push an agenda of propaganda to convince the people to destroy their own nation out of some false perceived righteousness and victimhood

17) They have failed to provide for the basic means of survival for their citizens while enslaving them in a system of fiat debt.

18) They have allowed private banks to create and in effect print money via loan schemes enlarging the total amount of money in circulation digitally and weakening the dollar for all Americans.

19) They have through legal and financial
persecution attempted to combat the
peoples First Amendment when the speech
employed is against the government
narrative and propaganda.

20) They have endeavored to destroy the free
and independent press through actions of
the courts and their allies in corporate
media, allowing entertainment to be
branded as the News and Press, allowing
state and corporate propaganda to be
disseminated as factual truth, whilst not
extending the same constitutional
protections as required to private citizen
press and independent free press.

21) They have attempted to create a state
religion in the forms of Liberal Socialism
and Atheism whereby the state is perceived
as Sovereign and Not the people.

22) They have attempted to guide the individual
religious beliefs of the people through Tax
Free laws where to qualify as a tax free
church or place of worship the place must

agree to not preach against government
wrongs and perpetuate government
propaganda.

23) They have in direct violation of the peoples
Bill of Rights infringed on the peoples right
of firearms ownership and private militia
formation through laws and acts that
prevent constitutional carry and defense,
and the gathering and training of militia
without approval or oversight of the state
even during times of peace

24) They have in many districts forced
Americans to employ extra steps and
burdens in order to "freely" exercise their
rights entitled to them at Birth and not of or
from government

25) They have failed to secure the national
borders as required by the Constitution
putting the nations people and economy at
risk of collapse

26) They have failed to provide for a
functioning system of immigration or to
enforce laws which would allow for a

functioning system of immigration causing untold numbers of illegal entries from less developed nations per year, back logged courts and citizenship programs, and pricing citizenship beyond the means of most immigrants forcing illegal entry in hopes of relocating a new voting base in America which being less educated and capable than the citizens here would be more manageable and gullible for the government to control further subverting the Natural Born Citizens will.

27) They have allowed for "And" aided through legislation and internal congressional rules corporate and lobbyist interest to control the central government through campaign financing and funding thus removing the peoples will from the rudders of government

28) They have spent frivolously the peoples lives and money on foreign entanglements, as well as banker and corporate foreign involvement never providing any true benefit or boon to the people of America

29) They have in coordination with central
banks and foreign powers endeavored to
create an atmosphere of worldwide terror
and conflict to further the destabilization of
these fifty States sovereignty and
economies

30) They have used policing actions around the
world to subvert the congressional power to
declare war and grant the executive
unilateral military power

31) They have frivolously wasted American
lives, wealth, and resources policing a
world order not in the interest of the people
of America

32) They have allowed the growth of the
executive branch to be near reaching
dictator status through the use of and
congressional allowance for Executive
Orders, National Security Directives and
mandates, and Presidential Decree.

33) They have undertaken actions, research,
intelligence gathering, societal engineering,
and both political and national interference
abroad that would otherwise be illegal at

home and endangers the image and person of American Citizens both at home and abroad

34) They have failed to develop this countries resources, endangering the American people, their sovereignty and their economy, by making us dependent on foreign sources of resources and goods

35) They have failed to maintain infrastructure, security, and interior of the nations roads, grounds, rails, ports, electrical grid, bridges, and airports

36) They have failed, by choice, to advance infrastructure for advancing technologies to all parts of the country in an attempt to force people from the land and into the cities where they are easier to monitor and control

37) They have supported the creation of monopolies and corporate oligarchies instead of promoting the peoples capitalist free market

38) They have supported and enforced foreign
treaties and agreements which were never
ratified by our Senate as required by the
Constitution and place an untoward burden
on the people and their economy forcing the
means of production to leave this country
for foreign soil increasing our dependence
on the globalist world economy

39) They have established a three tier justice
system where there is one level for the
connected and affiliated, one level for the
rich, and one for the rest of America

40) They have created within the judicial
system and greater society at large
ignorance of the true powers of the jury and
even allow the prosecution or state to
falsely instruct the jury on its prudence,
while at the same time punishing the
defense or people if they instruct the jury of
the truth even so far as declaring a miss
trial. The truth that the jury can nullify via
verdict any law, statute, or sentencing for
any reason. It is one of the three
metaphorical boxes of the peoples powers,
the Ballot Box, the Jury Box, and the
Cartridge Box.

41) They have in the pursuit of investigations engaged in acts of civil asset forfeiture and made the return of those assets even when found not guilty to be a tedious and involved process requiring the expenditure of additional resources to get back what was already one's own property

42) They do not have the power of income tax in the constitution and have failed to amend themselves that power knowing it would not pass the will of the people, so the act of congress creating the income tax system and the IRS is a voluntary act, and should you not partake in the system it is not compulsory only for those who file, but they have made property ownership and private loan acquisition to be dependent on your filed tax revenue making the taking part in society impossible without paying income taxes thus forcing compulsory income tax on the people outside of the Constitution

43) They have instituted a system of taxation whereby they tax every aspect of the peoples lives from property, sales,

purchases, utility usage, medical services, every time we transact money be it professionally or privately

44) They have repeatedly used the Tax Arm of the government the IRS, Internal Revenue Service, to persecute American Citizens for political ideology, political support, and political actions

45) When unable to use criminal or financial attacks to stop citizen activism or the truth from getting to the people they have smeared American citizens publicly and perversely in the media

46) They have failed to relinquish lands rightfully belonging to many states to those states and instead force those states to negotiate with a federal bureau of land management for lands that the Constitution specifically addresses should go to those states when state hood was acquired

47) They have failed to provide proper and adequate care for those veterans harmed in their proxy wars around the world

48) They have made a condition for enlistment in the armed services, which is supposed to be a volunteer service as standing armies were not originally in the constitution, the waving of certain rights to control over ones bodies especially in regards to vaccinations and other experimental procedures

49) They have outside the constitution provided themselves with the power of prohibition and censor and have created agencies to police these unconstitutionally stolen powers

50) They have failed to police corruption in the halls of government in regards to pay for play schemes in foreign aid, foreign and corporate investments, and insider trading, and even have instead created funds from tax payer money to pay out settlements for elected officials

51) They have spied on American Citizens violating the 4th and 5th amendments of the citizens Bill of Rights

52) They have falsely imprisoned American citizens entrapped by the government in a false flag maneuver on January Sixth 2020 and have violated those citizens 6th amendment right to speedy trial in an attempt to coerce these citizens into a guilty plea to justify the government narrative of insurrection. This is cruel and unusual punishment of the free citizens of this country by the central government.

53) They violate the security and future of this nation and its people by colluding with corporate think tanks, and private organizational steering committees such as but not limited to Bilderburg, Davos, World Economic Forum, Council on Foreign Ralations, and the Trilateral Commission to name a few

54) They openly promote treason called the New World Order whereby American Sovereignty is surpassed for a global corporate oligarchy

55) They pass legislation without ever reading it simply because the lobbyist and corporations fund them to do so

56) They pass legislation which only the people
are subject to, not they themselves in
government

57) They have orchestrated the political
campaigning system to allow for corporate,
and super pack control of the election
financing in this country instead of the
individual registered voters donations
making the elected politicians beholden to
corporations and lobbyist instead of the
constituency

58) They have orchestrated or prevented to stop
by choice election fraud, election meddling,
election interference, and election theft
stealing the peoples nation and future

59) They have allowed children to be attacked
and groomed by criminal elements of
society while endeavoring to cover up such
crimes when committed by connected elites
of the central government system

60) They break their own laws on secrecy
keeping facts and truths from the American
people under the guise of national security

but in truth to continue covering up their own corruption and law breaking

61) They favor nepotism as they funnel lucrative government contracts to family businesses and family members to key government positions or contacts

62) They have poisoned our waterways and supplies whilst also doing irreversible harm to the environment

63) They have persecuted free and independently living Americans solely for not being part of the corporate utility monopoly

64) They funded the research of a virus on foreign soil that was then released by that nation to destroy the world and Americas economy so as to make us more dependent on foreign sources of goods

65) They fund and perform Bio Weapons research abroad from this country that is illegal in this country as well as internationally through approved international agreements

66) They have operated black market drug rings
and trafficking to fund off book or black
operations and to entrap the people of
America in a state of addiction

67) They have armed our enemies against us

68) They have failed to police American
equipment when leaving foreign
entanglement making our enemies stronger
and us weaker, while also defrauding the
American people of the investment in such
equipment

69) They have orchestrated theater wars to push
a globalist agenda not in the interest of the
United States people

70) They continuously attempt to subvert the
Constitution they are sworn to follow in an
endeavor to abolish it and force these free
States and people under a system of
absolute despotism and one party rule

Treason is not what we do here this day but instead patriotism. It is the tyranny of the Washington Establishment Government which is treasonous and disruptive of the peace and prosperity both at home and abroad. We do not seek to depose the Constitution or the Union of the United States, but instead seek to restore the sovereignty of the Citizenry, the States, and the Constitution, as well as to embolden the Constitution so as to prevent this need again in the future.

We have attempted to assemble for redress to be beaten back, we have gone to the courts to have them stacked against us, we have gone to the agencies and seen the depth of the deep state and are left with no recourse but to declare the illegitimacy of the Washington DC Establishment Government and rebuke now by the greatest of Rights that of self governance and determination their subversion of our Constitution and will of the people.

Let the world be advised those who stand with the unconstitutional tyrants in Washington DC stand against the People of America.

End New Declaration

I do not say we should stand up to the government with arms. I believe that we should do so through the States governments and the courts while some jurisdictions are free. That said I have listed seventy potential grievances with the central government in Washington DC. Even if you don't support or agree with all of them in their entirety or in part if you do agree with more than Twenty Seven then you agree there are more grievances today than there were at the founding of this nation. Maybe you even have a grievance or two not in the above list. You also agree that this nation is divided. You agree that the central government, the Establishment Government in DC is to blame in part or in whole for the present state of affairs today in America. Lastly you agree that they the government do bear the responsibility.

What do we do with this information?

Take back your local governments by supporting candidates who align with your political desires. Then move to the State level. Push for amendments to strengthen the Constitution. Spend more time staying up to date and informed on topics that matter to you and general News and politics. Inform your neighbors. Call your elected representatives and let them know how you feel about topics. Write them as well or email. Be more active is step one. From there you will hopefully find your way as well as like minded individuals to work with. Move to states and jurisdictions that align with your views and needs. Maybe even run for office? If you choose to act then the choices are limitless. Choose to do nothing and the choices grow ever limited.

Remember this nation was founded on religion and politics. It is government propaganda which has made it a stigma that the topics of politics and religion are the things you don't talk about in polite society. Truth is they do not want us talking about these topics as they cause political ideological growth, the spreading of facts and truths, and the bringing together of like minded people. It also makes us more engaged and involved in day to day life and happenings around us. If our founding fathers had not discussed, debated, and argued politics and religion America today would not exist.

History is filled with nations where the government became more and more despotic. We know what happens when the peoples press is manipulated, free speech is denied, self protection and weapons ownership is prohibited, and the systems of due process done away with. Our world is built on the graves, bones, and ashes of those who suffered

such injustice for us, humanity to have come so far
to create the Republic of America on the ideals of
equality and basic rights and sovereignty. It's ours
to lose as they say. So act and try to win or don't
and lose by default. We are born free, but that
freedom comes at the cost of constant vigilance
and action.

Chapter 6; How would I embolden the
Constitution?

The way to strengthen the Constitution is by the
amendment process. Some amendments topics I
would be open to working on are:

1) Balanced Budget requirements
2) Term Limits
3) Restrictions on Congressional purview and
   rules
4) All laws passed must apply to the people
   and the government equally
5) Specie requirements and debt
6) Foreign entanglements and foreign aid
7) Immigration and the border
8) The Judiciary and the size of the Supreme
   Court
9) Income Tax, yes or no?
10) Regulatory, Intelligence and law
    enforcement agency oversight

11) Congressional oversight
12) Election requirements for heads of federal agencies and oversight boards
13) Conflict of Interest
14) Working with Civilian and Corporate think tanks
15) Come up with your own topic of change

How you choose to use this information is ultimately up to the individual reader. I only hope I may have opened your eyes to the complex times we live in and the sheer magnitude of the problems facing us as well as the dark dystopian future of global tyranny we risk if we do nothing. Research the topics contained within. Educate yourself and arm your mind with the knowledge of the true world we live in. Act on your conscience.

Appendix A

Original Declaration of Independence

In Congress, July 4, 1776

The unanimous Declaration of the thirteen united States of America, When in the Course of human events, it becomes necessary for one people to dissolve the political bands which have connected them with another, and to assume among the powers of the earth, the separate and equal station to which the Laws of Nature and of Nature's God entitle them, a decent respect to the opinions of mankind requires that they should declare the causes which impel them to the separation.

We hold these truths to be self-evident, that all men are created equal, that they are endowed by their Creator with certain unalienable Rights, that among these are Life, Liberty and the pursuit of Happiness.--That to secure these rights, Governments are instituted among Men, deriving their just powers from the consent of the governed, --That whenever any Form of Government becomes destructive of these ends, it is the Right of the People to alter or to abolish it, and to institute new Government, laying its foundation on such principles and organizing its powers in such form,

as to them shall seem most likely to effect their
Safety and Happiness. Prudence, indeed, will
dictate that Governments long established should
not be changed for light and transient causes; and
accordingly all experience hath shewn, that
mankind are more disposed to suffer, while evils
are sufferable, than to right themselves by
abolishing the forms to which they are accustomed.
But when a long train of abuses and usurpations,
pursuing invariably the same Object evinces a
design to reduce them under absolute Despotism, it
is their right, it is their duty, to throw off such
Government, and to provide new Guards for their
future security.--Such has been the patient
sufferance of these Colonies; and such is now the
necessity which constrains them to alter their
former Systems of Government. The history of the
present King of Great Britain is a history of
repeated injuries and usurpations, all having in
direct object the establishment of an absolute
Tyranny over these States. To prove this, let Facts
be submitted to a candid world.

He has refused his Assent to Laws, the most
wholesome and necessary for the public good.

He has forbidden his Governors to pass Laws of
immediate and pressing importance, unless
suspended in their operation till his Assent should
be obtained; and when so suspended, he has utterly
neglected to attend to them.

He has refused to pass other Laws for the
accommodation of large districts of people, unless

those people would relinquish the right of Representation in the Legislature, a right inestimable to them and formidable to tyrants only.

He has called together legislative bodies at places unusual, uncomfortable, and distant from the depository of their public Records, for the sole purpose of fatiguing them into compliance with his measures.

He has dissolved Representative Houses repeatedly, for opposing with manly firmness his invasions on the rights of the people.

He has refused for a long time, after such dissolutions, to cause others to be elected; whereby the Legislative powers, incapable of Annihilation, have returned to the People at large for their exercise; the State remaining in the mean time exposed to all the dangers of invasion from without, and convulsions within.

He has endeavoured to prevent the population of these States; for that purpose obstructing the Laws for Naturalization of Foreigners; refusing to pass others to encourage their migrations hither, and raising the conditions of new Appropriations of Lands.

He has obstructed the Administration of Justice, by refusing his Assent to Laws for establishing Judiciary powers.

He has made Judges dependent on his Will alone, for the tenure of their offices, and the amount and payment of their salaries.

He has erected a multitude of New Offices, and sent hither swarms of Officers to harrass our people, and eat out their substance.

He has kept among us, in times of peace, Standing Armies without the Consent of our legislatures.

He has affected to render the Military independent of and superior to the Civil power.

He has combined with others to subject us to a jurisdiction foreign to our constitution, and unacknowledged by our laws; giving his Assent to their Acts of pretended Legislation:

For Quartering large bodies of armed troops among us:

For protecting them, by a mock Trial, from punishment for any Murders which they should commit on the Inhabitants of these States:

For cutting off our Trade with all parts of the world:

For imposing Taxes on us without our Consent:

For depriving us in many cases, of the benefits of Trial by Jury:

For transporting us beyond Seas to be tried for pretended offences

For abolishing the free System of English Laws in a neighbouring Province, establishing therein an Arbitrary government, and enlarging its Boundaries so as to render it at once an example and fit instrument for introducing the same absolute rule into these Colonies:

For taking away our Charters, abolishing our most valuable Laws, and altering fundamentally the Forms of our Governments:

For suspending our own Legislatures, and declaring themselves invested with power to legislate for us in all cases whatsoever.

He has abdicated Government here, by declaring us out of his Protection and waging War against us.

He has plundered our seas, ravaged our Coasts, burnt our towns, and destroyed the lives of our people.

He is at this time transporting large Armies of foreign Mercenaries to compleat the works of death, desolation and tyranny, already begun with circumstances of Cruelty & perfidy scarcely paralleled in the most barbarous ages, and totally unworthy the Head of a civilized nation.

He has constrained our fellow Citizens taken Captive on the high Seas to bear Arms against their Country, to become the executioners of their friends and Brethren, or to fall themselves by their Hands.

He has excited domestic insurrections amongst us, and has endeavoured to bring on the inhabitants of our frontiers, the merciless Indian Savages, whose known rule of warfare, is an undistinguished destruction of all ages, sexes and conditions.

In every stage of these Oppressions We have Petitioned for Redress in the most humble terms: Our repeated Petitions have been answered only by repeated injury. A Prince whose character is thus marked by every act which may define a Tyrant, is unfit to be the ruler of a free people.

Nor have We been wanting in attentions to our Brittish brethren. We have warned them from time to time of attempts by their legislature to extend an unwarrantable jurisdiction over us. We have reminded them of the circumstances of our emigration and settlement here. We have appealed to their native justice and magnanimity, and we have conjured them by the ties of our common kindred to disavow these usurpations, which, would inevitably interrupt our connections and correspondence. They too have been deaf to the voice of justice and of consanguinity. We must, therefore, acquiesce in the necessity, which denounces our Separation, and hold them, as we hold the rest of mankind, Enemies in War, in Peace Friends.

We, therefore, the Representatives of the united States of America, in General Congress, Assembled, appealing to the Supreme Judge of the world for the rectitude of our intentions, do, in the

Name, and by Authority of the good People of
these Colonies, solemnly publish and declare, That
these United Colonies are, and of Right ought to be
Free and Independent States; that they are
Absolved from all Allegiance to the British Crown,
and that all political connection between them and
the State of Great Britain, is and ought to be totally
dissolved; and that as Free and Independent States,
they have full Power to levy War, conclude Peace,
contract Alliances, establish Commerce, and to do
all other Acts and Things which Independent States
may of right do. And for the support of this
Declaration, with a firm reliance on the protection
of divine Providence, we mutually pledge to each
other our Lives, our Fortunes and our sacred
Honor.

Georgia

Button Gwinnett

Lyman Hall

George Walton

North Carolina

William Hooper

Joseph Hewes

John Penn

South Carolina

Edward Rutledge

Thomas Heyward, Jr.

Thomas Lynch, Jr.

Arthur Middleton

Massachusetts

John Hancock

Maryland

Samuel Chase

William Paca

Thomas Stone

Charles Carroll of Carrollton

Virginia

George Wythe

Richard Henry Lee

Thomas Jefferson

Benjamin Harrison

Thomas Nelson, Jr.

Francis Lightfoot Lee

Carter Braxton

Pennsylvania

Robert Morris

Benjamin Rush

Benjamin Franklin

John Morton

George Clymer

James Smith

George Taylor

James Wilson

George Ross

Delaware

Caesar Rodney

George Read

Thomas McKean

New York

William Floyd

Philip Livingston

Francis Lewis

Lewis Morris

New Jersey

Richard Stockton

John Witherspoon

Francis Hopkinson

John Hart

Abraham Clark

New Hampshire

Josiah Bartlett

William Whipple

Massachusetts

Samuel Adams

John Adams

Robert Treat Paine

Elbridge Gerry

Rhode Island

Stephen Hopkins

William Ellery

Connecticut

Roger Sherman

Samuel Huntington

William Williams

Oliver Wolcott

New Hampshire

Matthew Thornton

Appendix B Sources and Citations

Harvard.edu

Southern Poverty Law Center

 US National Debt Clock

LostPine (www.LostPine.com)

Carl von Clausewitz – book entitled - "On War"

National Archives (www.archives.gov)

New York Times

New York Post

Washington Post

Infowars (www.infowars.com)

<u>**Appendix C Suggested Reading**</u>

The Historical Documents and Books including but not limited to:

The Declaration of Independence

The Constitution of the United States

The Articles of Confederation

The Federalist Papers

The Silence Dogood Letters

Thomas Paine's Common Sense

John Locke's Two Treatises on Government

Locke's Second Treatises on Government

Mark Twain book Roughing It

Emerich de Vattel book The Law of Nations

The Auto Biography of Ben Franklyn

Adam Smith book The Wealth of Nations

Abraham Lincoln The Gettysburg Address

Tranquillus book The Twelve Caesars

Modern Publications and Research

Lock Step by the Rockefeller Foundation

Rosa Koire book Behind the Green Mask UN
Agenda 21

Council on Foreign Relations Publications found at
www.cfrpublications.com

The Trilateral Commission Publications found at
www.trilateral.org/publications

Agenda 21 Department of Economic and Social
Affairs found at

Agenda 21 | Department of Economic and Social
Affairs (un.org)

G. Edward Griffin book The Creature from Jekyll
Island: A Second Look at the Federal Reserve

Ron Paul book End the Fed

Danielle DiMartino Booth book Fed Up; An
Insiders Take on Why the Federal Reserve is bad
for America